The Chase Through Mrs. Remraf's Kitchen

ELIZABETH NGOZI ADONU

F

Flowers Publications

United Kingdom • Germany

Educators, parents and libraries: for a variety of children's reading resources and support, visit:

The Smart Reading Child Project

www.smartreadingchild.com

ISBN-13: 978-1479166824
ISBN-10: 1479166820

www.flowerspublications.com | www.flowersbooks.com

DEDICATION

To the memory of my Dad *-Godson Udensi Okpara -* who stimulated the childhood passion for reading in me.

Also to every parent who is willing and committed to inspiring and supporting children towards developing the discipline and passion for reading.

ACKNOWLEDGMENTS

Certain wonderful individuals deserve my appreciation and gratitude:

Dr. Joseph Adonu (my husband and companion) whose pedagogy and words of encouragement spurred me on to launch the Smart Reading Child Project, of which this book is part.

Dexter and Zanetor, my two loving children, whose great interest in books constantly motivates me into concocting our very own bedtime stories, and for always being the first to listen to and read through my stories, freely giving me their honest and priceless opinions.

Michael and Melanie Flowers (Germany) whose invaluable friendship and technical support facilitated the design and publishing of this book.

Everyone at Greenhouse Mentoring, Wigmore Library, Someries Infant and Junior Schools (all in Luton, England) where my involvement in work and volunteering has enriched my experience and inspiration towards completing this book.

Finally, *Soli Deo Gloria.*

Help Your Child To Read!

This book is designed and written to support, motivate and encourage children to read. It uses simple everyday language based on common behavioural reactions in daily activities from children to situations around them. It also takes into account the intellectual, social, emotional and moral developmental needs of children.

By using visually-captivating illustrations and real-life activities, the story draws on common experiences to create scenarios intended to inculcate cherished values of life in children while stimulating their curiosity towards passionate reading.

Read regularly with your child. Reading helps build confidence and a sense of efficacy in children and can be a source of fun. As you go through the pages, look at the pictures and talk about what you see.

For more information and update on supporting children's reading, visit:

www.smartreadingchild.com

.

The Chase Through
Mrs. Remraf's Kitchen

Mr. Remraf looked out of the kitchen window and noticed that the weather was changing.

There was a thick dark cloud lurking in the sky. "I had better get the children to help me gather the animals inside safely before the rains come," he thought. Just at that instant he saw a horse and a pig running past the window.

Then he craned his neck and saw a dog. It was his dog, Digger. Digger was chasing his horse and pig.

"Shifty shenanigans!" he cried out. "What on earth is happening?"

Before he could think of an answer, he saw his children, Timmy, Sammy and their sister Clammy run fast past the windows with four turkeys in hot pursuit.

"I think I should go out now and see what is happening," Mr. Remraf said to himself.

He left the food he was eating, took his long '*shooing stick*', grabbed a hat and nearly knocked down Mrs. Remraf as he charged through the door. "Where are you going in a hurry? You have not finished your food," cried Mrs. Remraf, but Mr. Remraf was already gone.

Inside the kitchen, Mrs. Remraf opened the washing machine and started taking out the washing one at a time.

She took out Sammy's school trousers and looked at it thinking, "My, oh my, this pair is getting too small for Sammy, he surely needs a new one."

As she stretched her hand to drop the trousers in the laundry bucket, she heard a running noise. "Neigh, neigh, Neeiiighhh" cried the horse as he ran through the kitchen and out the living room door, carrying with him Sammy's washed trousers.

"Shifty shenanigans! What on earth is this? A horse in my kitchen?" screamed Mrs. Remraf.

No sooner had Mrs. Remraf gathered herself and picked another item of clothing than she heard another running sound. She took a look at the door and at Clammy's skirt in her hands and seemed to be deciding what to do when in charged the pig.

"Oink, oink, oooiiinnnk," cried the pig as he ran past Mrs. Remraf through the kitchen and out the living room door, carrying with him Clammy's skirt.

Mrs. Remraf blinked and continued picking out the laundry. She took a green jumper which belonged to Timmy and shook it in the air. She was just about to drop it in the bucket when she heard yet another running sound and in came Digger the dog.

Digger stopped, gave three barks and reached out to Mrs. Remraf almost as if he expected her to hand over the green jumper.

Digger waited patiently, but when Mrs. Remraf made no attempt to give him the jumper, he leapt up and collected it.

He ran through the kitchen and out the living room door. A speechless Mrs. Remraf was now totally confused. She straightened up, rubbed her eyes and stretched her arms widely and then continued with her job, fully conscious and ready for the next laundry snatching.

She took out Mr. Remraf's garden overalls from the washing machine and held it with both hands, inspecting it. Without any warning, Timmy, Sammy and Clammy charged into the kitchen, hoisting the laundry bucket and falling onto Mrs. Remraf in a big muddle.

"Shifty Shenanigans!" screeched Mrs. Remraf as the three children collected themselves up and ran through the kitchen and out the living room door, carrying the bucket.

No sooner had they gone out of sight than four very noisy turkeys come following.

This time, Mrs. Remraf reached for the washing machine quickly and brought out four little pairs of shorts. She handed one to each turkey and sank to the floor as the turkeys ran off through the kitchen and out the living room door, the shorts in their beaks.

Mrs. Remraf started to cry, "My washing is all ruined, what a terrible mess."

"Now I will not be able to do my ironing, and there will be no time to pick the fruits and make the jams!" She reached for a tissue to dab the tears from her face and looked up in horror.

"Shifty Shenanigans, not you too Mr. Remraf!" she cried, "Charging through my kitchen and messing up my laundry!"

"Sorry, Mrs. R," said Mr. Remraf, "I can't stop for a chat this minute. I am chasing the turkeys that chased Timmy, Sammy and Clammy, who chased Digger, who chased the pig, that chased the horse, that was chasing the clouds."

With that he vamoosed through the door.

Mrs. Remraf stood up and thought for a while. She was hatching a plan just in case there was a second invasion of her kitchen. "Ah ha!" she cried with excitement as she walked to the cabinet where they kept the horse's biscuits.

She brought out lots of biscuits and made a trail from the kitchen, through the living room and all the way to the horse's barn.

She waited. She made sure that she followed the same trail made from the earlier chase, except this time she was going to divert the horse into continuing on the biscuit trail in order to lure it into the barn. Mrs. Remraf didn't have to wait for long. She heard a running sound which seemed to follow the trail. As the sound got closer, she ran for the barn, dropping more biscuits to continue the trail. The horse noticed and followed, running straight into the barn.

Mrs. Remraf jumped up from behind the door where she was hiding and quickly bolted it.

"Mission done! No more shifty shenanigans in my kitchen, Mr. Neigh!" she said, walking back with satisfaction into the kitchen for her next culprit.

She walked to the cabinet once again and this time opened it to get some nibbles for the pig. She brought out lots of them and made a trail from the kitchen, through the living room and all the way to the pig's sty. She waited.

She made sure that she followed the same trail made from the earlier chase, except once again she was going to divert the pig into continuing on the nibbles trail, in order to lure it into the sty. Mrs. Remraf didn't have to wait for long. She heard a running sound which seemed to follow the trail. As the sound got closer, she ran for the sty, dropping more nibbles to continue the trail. The pig noticed and followed, running straight into the sty.

Mrs. Remraf jumped up from behind the door, where she was hiding and quickly bolted it. "Mission done! No more shifty shenanigans in my kitchen, Mr. Oinky!" she said, walking with satisfaction back into the kitchen for her next culprit.

Mrs. Remraf walked to the cabinet where they kept the dog's food and reached for some fruit clusters. She mistakenly picked a packet of horse biscuits. Mrs. Remraf chuckled and put it right back when she discovered her error.

She brought out lots of fruit clusters and made a trail from the kitchen, through the living room and all the way to Digger's kennel. Once again she waited. Just as previously, she made sure that she followed the same trail made from the earlier chase, with the plan to divert Digger into continuing on the fruit cluster trail, in order to lure him into the kennel.

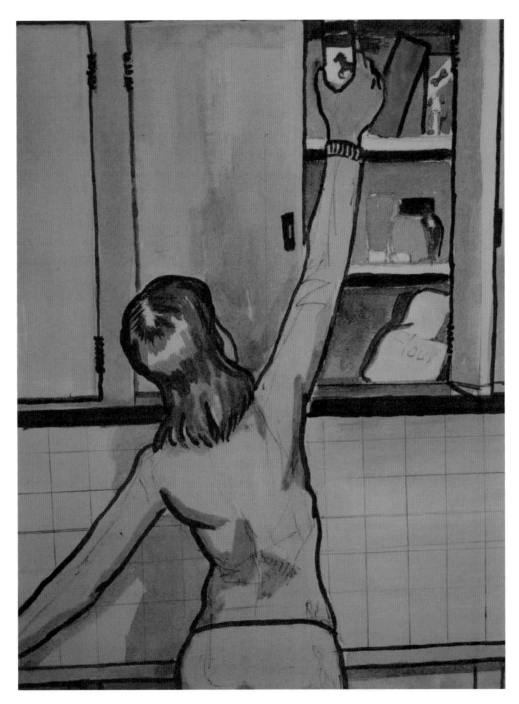

Mrs. Remraf didn't have to wait for long. She heard a running sound which seemed to follow the trail. As the sound got closer, she ran for the kennel, dropping more fruit clusters to continue the trail. Digger noticed and followed, running at full speed straight into the kennel.

Mrs. Remraf jumped up from behind the kennel where she was hiding and quickly bolted it. "Mission done! No more shifty shenanigans in my kitchen, Mr. Digger!" she said, walking with satisfaction back into the kitchen for her next culprit.

She went back to the kitchen and got busy, setting up for the children. She brought out some biscuits in a plate and set the plate on the kitchen table. She brought out three cups and filled them with apple juice. Now all she had to do was wait. Soon, in trudged Timmy, Sammy and Clammy, looking rather worn out with mud on their faces.

They stopped as they saw the table set for three.

"The animals can wait, time for a snack!" called out Timmy, as they all made their way to the sink, washed their hands and faces and settled in their chairs.

"Mission done! No more shifty shenanigans in my kitchen" Mrs. Remraf murmured, walking out of the kitchen for her next culprit.

She went outside through the back door of the kitchen, carrying some bird nuts. She sprinkled lots of them on the ground to form a trail from the door, all the way to the back of the house and into the turkey coop. Mrs. Remraf knew she didn't have to run for the turkeys to follow. She was convinced that they would freely 'peck their way' into the coop, and sure enough they did.

From her hiding place, she saw all four turkeys marching into the coop. Mrs. Remraf jumped up from her hiding place and quickly bolted the coop.

"Mission done! No more shifty shenanigans in my kitchen, turkey tails" she said, walking with satisfaction to the back of the kitchen.

She stood outside, behind the kitchen. She chose to position herself close to the kitchen door, with a laundry bucket filled with the washing that she managed to save. Mrs. Remraf was going to hand the bucket over to Mr. Remraf to hang out the washing, then go back and find him an empty laundry bucket for his second chore.

Mrs. Remraf had figured out that the best way to get Mr. Remraf was to stand outside the kitchen door and make sure that he didn't enter the kitchen. She stood whistling happily to herself. Suddenly, she looked up and saw Pitty, her cat, holding on to the trouser leg of a 'hatless' and 'stickless' Mr. Remraf and almost dragging him.

Pitty had found Mr. Remraf near the pear tree, tired and looking almost as if he had been duffed up by the animals. "Well done, Pitty, jumbo cat snack for you tonight!" she said as she patted Pitty on the head. She looked at her husband and said "Hello Mr. Remraf, we meet again. This time, I can't allow you to stop for a chat or a snack or even a '*sit*' !" She handed the first bucket to Mr. Remraf who walked away to hang the clothes. Mr. Remraf returned for the second bucket, turned and started walking around, looking for the scattered and muddy laundry that would need washing all over again.

"Pitty and I will have some rest now. We have had enough shifty shenanigans to last us a year!" Mrs. Remraf smiled as she made herself a nice cup of vanilla flavoured red bush tea and got out some jumbo cat snacks for Pitty.

"Miiaaaooooow!" cheered Pitty, smiling.

THE END

GLOSSARY

Barn: An outbuilding or structure on a farm used to shelter livestock.

Bolted: Past tense for 'bolt': Secure a door or gate using a sliding bar that fits into a socket.

Conscious: Awake and responsive.

Coop: An enclosure or hut in which poultry is kept.

Craned: Past tense of 'crane': Stretch the neck in order to get a better view of something.

Culprit: Somebody or something responsible for a problem.

Divert: Change the route or path taken by something or someone.

Duffed up: Beaten up.

Hatching: Secretly devising a plot, plan, or scheme.

Invasion: Entry without invitation.

Kennel: A small outdoor structure like a hut, built for a dog to sleep in.

Lure: Persuade somebody or something to go somewhere or do something by offering something tempting.

Lurking: Waiting in a concealed position or a shadowy corner.

Muddle: Mix things together in a confused way.

Murmured: Say something very quietly.

Nibbles: Small quick bites or eating something in a series of small quick bites.

Pursuit: The act of going after somebody or something.

Shenanigans: A playful trick.

Shifty: Something not to be trusted.

Sty: A house for a pig.

Trudged: Slow, heavy walk.

Vamoose: Leave in a hurried way.

ABOUT THE AUTHOR

Elizabeth Ngozi Adonu rose from a background of Health and Psychology and has great interest in children's development. She believes in the need to invest in children's educational, social, emotional and moral development as the basis for their achievement and fulfillment in life, being the future leaders of our world.

Her passion for children and young people's holistic development stemmed from an inspired involvement with children and the youth in various capacities: being a parent, mentoring and mentor supervision, tutoring children with autism, co-ordinating and overseeing homework activities in various local libraries, offering training and support in children's anger management and serving as a school governor.

Elizabeth holds a Bachelor's Degree in Nursing and Psychology, as well as a Master's Degree in Occupational Health and Safety Management. She is married to Dr. Joseph Adonu (a social psychologist) and they have two children -Dexter and Zanetor- with whom she lives in England.

19522143R00034

Printed in Poland
by Amazon Fulfillment
Poland Sp. z o.o., Wrocław